I am a
Red Panda

Alexis Roumanis

LET'S READ
AV2
BY WEIGL™
ADDED VALUE • AUDIO VISUAL

www.av2books.com

Go to **www.av2books.com**,
and enter this book's
unique code.

BOOK CODE

H188167

AV² by Weigl brings you media
enhanced books that support
active learning.

AV² provides enriched content that supplements and complements this book. Weigl's AV² books
strive to create inspired learning and engage young minds in a total learning experience.

Your AV² Media Enhanced books come alive with...

Audio
Listen to sections of
the book read aloud.

Video
Watch informative
video clips.

Embedded Weblinks
Gain additional information
for research.

Try This!
Complete activities and
hands-on experiments.

Key Words
Study vocabulary, and
complete a matching
word activity.

Quizzes
Test your knowledge.

Slide Show
View images and
captions, and prepare
a presentation.

... and much, much more!

Published by AV² by Weigl
350 5th Avenue, 59th Floor   New York, NY   10118
Websites: www.av2books.com   www.weigl.com

Library of Congress Control Number: 2014934880
ISBN 978-1-4896-1274-8 (hardcover)
ISBN 978-1-4896-1275-5 (softcover)
ISBN 978-1-4896-1276-2 (single user eBook)
ISBN 978-1-4896-1277-9 (multi-user eBook)

Printed in the United States of America in North Mankato, Minnesota
1 2 3 4 5 6 7 8 9 0 18 17 16 15 14

042014
WEP150314

Senior Editor: Aaron Carr   Art Director: Terry Paulhus

Weigl acknowledges Getty Images as the primary image supplier for this title.

I am a Red Panda

In this book, I will teach you about

- myself
- my food
- my home
- my family

and much more!

I am a red panda.

I am the smallest kind of panda in the world.

7

I use my tail as a blanket when it is cold.

I spend most of
my time in trees.
I will even sleep in trees.

I had grey hair
when I was a baby.
My hair turned red when
I was four months old.

I spend half of my day eating bamboo.

15

I use my tail
to keep from falling.

16

17

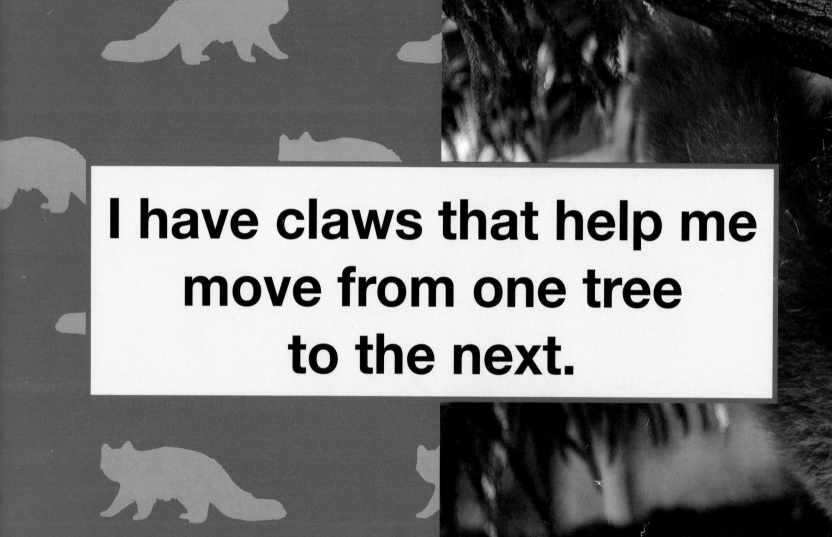

I have claws that help me move from one tree to the next.

18

I live in the
mountains of Asia.

I am a red panda.

RED PANDA FACTS

These pages provide detailed information that expands on the interesting facts found in the book. They are intended to be used by adults as a learning support to help young readers round out their knowledge of each amazing animal featured in the *I Am* series.

Pages 4–5

I am a red panda. The red panda is a type of mammal. It is most closely related to weasels, badgers, raccoons, and skunks. The red panda is known for its striped tail, and red and white patterned face. No two have exactly the same fur pattern.

Pages 6–7

I am the smallest kind of panda in the world. Red pandas can reach a length of 24 inches (60 centimeters), while the giant panda can reach a length of 6 feet (1.8 meters). Even though they share the same name, red pandas are not closely related to giant pandas. The red panda got its name from the Nepalese name *nigalya ponya*, which means 'bamboo footed'. The red panda is the only living species in its family.

Pages 8–9

I use my tail as a blanket when it is cold. The red panda lives in mountainous areas, up to 16,400 feet (5,000 meters) above sea level. In this habitat, it can get cold and wet. To keep warm, the red panda has a long and thick coat. The red panda will wrap its tail around itself when it is very cold. The tail of a red panda can reach a length of 18 inches (46 centimeters).

Pages 10–11

I spend most of my time in trees. I will even sleep in trees. In the red panda's habitat, tree trunks are covered in red moss and white lichen. The red panda's red and white coat blends in with these trees, helping it to keep hidden from other animals. The red panda will climb to the top of a tree when it wants to sunbathe.

I had grey hair when I was a baby. My hair turned red when I was four months old. Baby red pandas are called cubs. Cubs are born with a thick coat of grey fur. When cubs are born, their eyes stay closed for about 2 to 3 weeks. During this time, mothers usually keep their cubs in a tree hollow. When the cubs are between 13 and 22 weeks old, the mother is finished nursing them. At this time, the cubs' fur will turn red.

I spend half of my day eating bamboo. Red pandas are herbivores. Ninety percent of their diet is made up of bamboo. They also eat eggs, fruit, and acorns. Bamboo is a safe food source for the red panda. Few other species eat bamboo, and it grows wild on mountainsides. Red pandas spend half of their waking hours eating bamboo because it is a low calorie food source.

I use my tail to keep from falling. A red panda's tail can be as long as its body. The long tail serves as a counterbalance. This is helpful when the red panda is walking on a narrow branch or climbing. The red panda will straighten out its tail when it is walking on the ground.

I have claws that help me move from one tree to the next. Red pandas have semi-retractable claws. These claws help the pandas to move from one branch to another with ease. An extension of the red panda's wrist bone acts as a thumb. This helps the red panda to hold onto branches while it moves. The thumb also helps the red panda to grasp its food.

I live in the mountains of Asia. I am a red panda. The red panda's natural habitat has decreased in size over the past several decades. Red pandas are also hunted. Scientists believe that the red panda population has declined by 30 percent over the past three generations. The red panda is a vulnerable species because there are fewer than 10,000 red pandas left in the world.

KEY WORDS

Research has shown that as much as 65 percent of all written material published in English is made up of 300 words. These 300 words cannot be taught using pictures or learned by sounding them out. They must be recognized by sight. This book contains 37 common sight words to help young readers improve their reading fluency and comprehension. This book also teaches young readers several important content words, such as proper nouns. These words are paired with pictures to aid in learning and improve understanding.

Page	Sight Words First Appearance	Page	Content Words First Appearance
4	a, am, I	4	red panda
6	in, kind, of, the, world	6	panda
8	as, is, it, my, use, when	8	blanket, tail
10	even, most, time, trees, will	12	baby, grey, hair, months, red
12	four, had, old, turned, was	14	bamboo, half
14	day	18	claws
16	from, keep, to	20	Asia
18	have, help, me, move, next, one, that		
20	live, mountains		

Check out av2books.com for activities, videos, audio clips, and more!

1 Go to av2books.com

2 Enter book code H188167

3 Explore your red panda book!

www.av2books.com